The Wealth Mindset: A Guide to Achieving Financial Freedom and Living the Life You Want

By
Michael Moran

Table of contents

Introduction

The Wealth Mindset: A Guide to Achieving Financial Freedom and Living the Life You Want is a comprehensive and actionable guide to developing a successful mindset and building wealth. This book explores the importance of taking control of your finances, creating a solid financial plan, and developing the right habits and attitudes to achieve financial freedom. It provides practical advice on managing money, reducing debt, saving for the future, and investing for growth. Whether you are just starting out on your financial journey or looking to make significant changes to your financial life, this book has something for everyone. With clear and concise explanations and real-life examples, The Wealth Mindset will help you unlock your full financial potential and live the life you've always wanted. Start reading now and take the first step towards achieving financial freedom and living life on your own terms.

Chapter 1

Understanding the importance of a wealth mindset

A wealth mindset is the way a person thinks and approaches money, work, and investments. It is the foundation of financial stability and success, and it is important for everyone to understand its significance. In this article, we will delve into what a wealthy mindset is, why it matters, and how you can cultivate one for yourself.

What is a Wealth Mindset?
A wealth mindset is the set of beliefs and attitudes that determine how a

person views and manages their money. It is the way a person perceives wealth and financial stability, and it affects their actions, decisions, and outcomes. People with a wealth mindset are proactive, disciplined, and focused on their financial goals. They believe that wealth is a result of hard work, smart decisions, and perseverance.

Why Does a Wealth Mindset Matter? A wealth mindset is crucial for financial stability and success. It determines how a person approaches money and investments, and it can greatly impact their financial outcomes. People with a wealth mindset are more likely to save, invest, and plan for the future. They are less likely to spend impulsively and make poor financial decisions. A wealth mindset also enables a person to be resilient in the face of financial setbacks and to bounce back from them more quickly.

How to Cultivate a Wealth Mindset Cultivating a wealth mindset is not difficult, but it does require discipline and a willingness to change old habits and beliefs. Here are some steps you can take to develop a wealth mindset:

Educate yourself: The first step to developing a wealth mindset is to educate yourself on financial matters. Read books, attend seminars, and seek advice from financial experts.

Set financial goals: Setting financial goals gives you a roadmap for your financial future. It helps you stay focused and motivated, and it provides you with a sense of direction.

Practice self-discipline: A wealth mindset requires discipline and self-control. This means resisting the urge to spend impulsively and making smart decisions about your money.

Surround yourself with positive influences: Surrounding yourself with positive, like-minded people can help you maintain a wealthy mindset. Seek out mentors and join communities of people who share your financial goals.

Stay positive: A positive attitude is crucial for cultivating a wealthy mindset. Believe in yourself and your ability to achieve financial success, and stay focused on your goals, even during difficult times.

Chapter 2

Identifying limiting beliefs and changing them

Limiting beliefs are negative thoughts and attitudes that hold us back from reaching our full potential. They are often rooted in past experiences, fear, and self-doubt, and they can prevent us from pursuing our dreams and achieving our goals. However, it is possible to identify and change these limiting beliefs to lead a more fulfilling life.

What are Limiting Beliefs?
Limiting beliefs are negative thoughts that we believe to be true about

ourselves, others, or the world. They can be as simple as believing that we are not good enough or smart enough to succeed, or as complex as believing that we will never be happy or find love. Limiting beliefs are often learned in childhood and reinforced throughout our lives, and they can be difficult to change.

Why it is Important to Identify Limiting Beliefs
Identifying limiting beliefs is important because they can hold us back from reaching our full potential. They can prevent us from pursuing our dreams, taking risks, and making positive changes in our lives. Limiting beliefs can also lead to

feelings of anxiety, depression, and low self-esteem. By identifying and changing these beliefs, we can overcome these challenges and lead a more fulfilling life.

How to Identify Limiting Beliefs
Identifying limiting beliefs can be challenging, but it is essential for personal growth and self-improvement. Here are some steps you can take to identify your limiting beliefs:

Reflect on your thoughts and feelings: Take time to reflect on your thoughts and feelings, especially when you are facing a difficult situation or decision. Ask yourself what you are telling yourself about the situation and whether these thoughts are positive or negative.

Examine your self-talk: Pay attention to the way you talk to yourself. Are you constantly criticizing yourself or putting yourself down? If so, these negative thoughts may be limiting beliefs.

Look at your past experiences: Think about past experiences that have shaped your beliefs and attitudes. Are there any experiences that have left a negative impact on you and influenced your beliefs about yourself or others?

Seek feedback from others: Seek feedback from people who know you well. Ask them what they believe are your strengths and weaknesses, and if they see any patterns in your thinking or behavior that may be limiting.

How to Change Limiting Beliefs
Once you have identified your limiting beliefs, the next step is to change them. This can be a challenging process, but it is essential for personal growth and self-improvement. Here are some steps you can take to change limiting beliefs:

Challenge your beliefs: Ask yourself whether your beliefs are really true. Are they based on evidence or just assumptions? By challenging your beliefs, you can gain a new perspective and start to see things differently.

Reframe your thoughts: Reframe your thoughts to be more positive and empowering. Instead of telling yourself that you are not good enough, for example, tell yourself that you are capable and deserving of success.

Practice positive self-talk: Practice speaking positively to yourself. This can be as simple as affirming yourself each day with positive statements or surrounding yourself with positive influences.

Surround yourself with positive influences: Surround yourself with positive, supportive people who believe in you and your abilities. Seek out mentorship and seek advice from those who have overcome similar challenges.

Take action: Finally, take action towards your goals. This can be a powerful way to change your beliefs and reinforce positive, empowering thoughts.

Chapter 3

Setting clear financial goals

Setting clear financial goals is an important step towards achieving financial stability and independence. Having specific, well-defined goals can help you prioritize your spending, make smart investment decisions, and stay motivated as you work towards your financial objectives. Here are some tips for setting and reaching your financial goals.

Determine your priorities: The first step in setting financial goals is to identify what is most important to you. Do you want to pay off debt, build an emergency fund, save for a down payment on a house, or something else? Make a list of your top financial priorities and rank them in order of importance.

Be specific: Vague goals, such as "save more money," can be difficult to measure and track. Instead, set specific, quantifiable goals. For example, "save $10,000 in an emergency fund by December 31st" is a much clearer and more achievable goal.

Set realistic expectations: It's important to set achievable goals that you can realistically reach in the timeframe you have set for yourself. For example, if you have a lot of high-interest debt, it may take longer to pay it off than you originally planned. Be honest with yourself about what you can realistically achieve, and adjust your goals as necessary.

Create a budget: Once you have set your financial goals, it's time to create a budget. A budget will help you track your income and expenses and see how much money you have left over each month to put towards your goals. It can also help you identify areas where you can cut back on spending so you can reach your goals more quickly.

Track your progress: Regularly tracking your progress towards your financial goals can help keep you motivated and on track. Consider setting up a spreadsheet or using a personal finance app to help you monitor your progress.

Celebrate your successes: Finally, be sure to celebrate your successes along the way. Whether it's paying off a credit card or reaching your emergency fund savings goal, take time to acknowledge your achievements and reward yourself for a job well done.

Stay flexible: Life can be unpredictable, so it's important to stay flexible and adjust your financial goals as needed. If your circumstances change, don't be afraid to reassess and adjust your goals.

Seek advice: If you're unsure about how to set financial goals or need help creating a plan, consider speaking to a financial advisor. They can provide you with valuable advice and help you create a comprehensive financial plan.

Chapter 4

Building an emergency fund

Building an emergency fund is a crucial step in financial planning. It provides a safety net for unexpected expenses, such as job loss, medical emergencies, or home repairs. Without an emergency fund, these unexpected events can quickly lead to financial stress and even debt.

An emergency fund is a critical component of a well-rounded financial plan. It provides a safety net to cover unexpected expenses, such as a medical emergency, job loss, or a major home repair, without having to rely on credit card debt or high-interest loans. Having an emergency fund in place can reduce financial stress and help you maintain financial stability, even during challenging times. Here are the steps to building an emergency fund:

Determine the size of your emergency fund: A common rule of thumb is to aim for three to six months of living expenses in an emergency fund. This amount may vary based on individual circumstances, such as job stability, health insurance coverage, and monthly expenses. Start by calculating your monthly expenses and multiplying that number by the number of months you want to cover in your emergency fund.

Open a dedicated savings account: Choose a savings account specifically for your emergency fund, separate from your regular checking account. This makes it easier to track your progress and reduces the temptation to use the funds for non-emergency expenses. Look for a high-yield savings account with a low minimum balance requirement and no monthly fees.

Automate your savings: Automating your emergency fund contributions by setting up a monthly transfer from your checking account to your emergency fund savings account can help you stay on track and make saving a habit. Start with a small amount and gradually increase it over time.

Prioritize your emergency fund: Make building your emergency fund a priority, especially when it comes to budgeting. Consider cutting back on discretionary expenses, such as dining out or entertainment, to redirect those funds to your emergency savings. You can also look for ways to increase your income, such as taking on a side job or selling items you no longer need.

Monitor your progress: Regularly review your emergency fund balance and adjust your contributions as needed to reach your target. Celebrate your progress and stay motivated by setting goals and tracking your progress.

Keep it liquid: An emergency fund should be easily accessible in case of an emergency, so choose a savings account that allows you to withdraw funds quickly without penalty.

Start small and be consistent. It may seem overwhelming to save several months' worth of expenses, but starting small and being consistent can help you reach your goal. Consider setting aside a specific amount each month, such as 10% of your income. You can also look for ways to cut back on expenses to free up more money for savings.

Keep your emergency fund in a separate account. Keeping your emergency fund in a separate account, such as a high-yield savings account, can help you avoid dipping into it for non-emergency expenses. This will also help you keep track of your progress and make sure the money is easily accessible when you need it.

Building an emergency fund takes time and discipline, but the peace of mind it provides is worth the effort. By taking steps to build and maintain an emergency fund, you can protect your financial security and ensure that unexpected expenses don't disrupt your finances.

Chapter 5

Developing a budget and sticking to it

Budgeting is an important aspect of personal finance that can help you control your spending, plan for your future and achieve your financial goals. Whether you are living on a fixed income or have multiple streams of income, having a budget can help you keep track of your expenses and ensure that you are not spending more than you earn. Here is a step-by-step guide on how to develop a budget and stick to it.

Step 1: Determine your income.

The first step in developing a budget is to determine your monthly income. This includes all sources of income, such as your salary, rental income, and any other sources of regular income. Make sure to include both your pre-tax and after-tax income, as this will give you a more accurate picture of how much money you have available each month.

Step 2: Track your spending.

The next step is to track your spending for a month. This will help you get an accurate idea of how much money you are spending each month and where your money is going. You can use a budgeting app, spreadsheet, or pen and paper to track your spending. Be sure to include all expenses, big and small, and categorize them into categories such as housing, food, transportation, entertainment, and others.

Step 3: Identify areas where you can cut back.

Once you have a clear idea of your income and expenses, you can start identifying areas where you can cut back on your spending. This might include reducing your dining out expenses, cutting back on your entertainment budget, or finding ways to reduce your monthly bills. The goal here is to reduce your spending so that it is less than your income.

Step 4: Set a budget.

With a clear idea of your income and expenses, you can now set a budget. Start by allocating money for your essential expenses such as housing, food, transportation, and utilities. Then, allocate money for your non-essential expenses such as entertainment, dining out, and others. Make sure that your budget is realistic and that you have enough money to cover your expenses and save for your future.

Review and adjust your budget regularly.

It is important to review and adjust your budget regularly to make sure that it is still realistic and that you are staying on track. Life is always changing, and your expenses will change as well, so it is important to make adjustments to your budget as needed.

Sticking to a budget takes discipline and commitment, but it is worth it in the long run. With a budget in place, you will have a better understanding of your financial situation and be able to make informed decisions about your spending and saving. So start today, develop a budget and stick to it, and you'll be on your way to a bright financial future

Chapter 6

Educating yourself on personal finance

Personal finance is an important aspect of life that affects our daily lives and our future prospects. Whether you are just starting out in your career or approaching retirement, it is never too early or too late to start educating yourself on personal finance. Here are some tips to help you get started.

Start by creating a budget.

A budget is a written plan for how you plan to spend your money. By creating a budget, you can get a better understanding of your income and expenses and identify areas where you can reduce your spending. This will help you to prioritize your spending and ensure that you have enough money left over to save and invest for the future.

Get to know your credit score.

Your credit score is an important factor in determining your ability to get loans, credit cards, and other financial products. It is important to monitor your credit score regularly and take steps to improve it if necessary. You can obtain a free credit report from the major credit reporting agencies once a year, and there are also a number of online resources that offer free credit monitoring services.

Learn about saving and investing.

Saving and investing are key components of personal finance. By setting aside money each month and investing it in a variety of financial products, you can build a nest egg for the future and grow your wealth over time. There are many resources available to help you learn about saving and investing, including books, websites, and courses.

Seek professional advice.

While it is important to educate yourself on personal finance, it is also a good idea to seek the advice of a professional financial advisor. A financial advisor can help you create a personalized financial plan and offer advice on specific financial products and strategies that may be appropriate for your situation.

Stay informed.

Personal finance is a constantly evolving field, and it is important to stay informed about changes and developments. You can do this by reading personal finance websites, following financial experts on social media, and subscribing to personal finance newsletters.

Chapter 7

Investing in your future

Investing in your future is a crucial step in securing a comfortable life for yourself and your family. Whether you're just starting out in your career or you're looking to plan for retirement, investing your money wisely can help you reach your financial goals and provide financial security for years to come.

There are many different types of investments to consider, including stocks, bonds, mutual funds, and real estate. Each type of investment comes with its own risks and rewards, so it's important to do your research and understand what you're getting into before making any decisions.

One of the most important things to keep in mind when investing is your timeline. If you're planning for retirement, you'll want to focus on long-term investments that have the potential to grow over time, such as stocks or mutual funds. On the other hand, if you're looking to invest for a shorter time period, you may want to consider bonds or other fixed-income investments that provide more stability and predictability.

Another important factor to consider when investing is your risk tolerance. If you're more conservative and don't want to take on too much risk, you may want to focus on investments like bonds or savings accounts. However, if you're willing to take on more risk for the potential of higher returns, you may want to consider investing in the stock market or other growth-oriented investments.

Regardless of your investment strategy, it's also important to diversify your portfolio. This means spreading your investments out across different types of assets and industries to reduce your overall risk and increase your chances of success.

Finally, one of the most important things you can do when investing in your future is to educate yourself. This means learning about different types of investments, understanding the risks and rewards involved, and staying up to date on market conditions and trends. You can also consider working with a financial advisor to help guide you in making informed investment decisions.

Chapter 8

Surrounding yourself with positive and supportive people

Surrounding Yourself with Positive and Supportive People: Why it Matters and How to Do it

As human beings, we are social creatures and our relationships with others greatly impact our lives. This is why surrounding ourselves with positive and supportive people is crucial for our mental, emotional, and even physical well-being. In this article, we will discuss why it is important to surround ourselves with positive and supportive people, and how we can achieve this.

Why Surrounding Yourself with Positive and Supportive People Matters

Boosts our self-esteem: When we surround ourselves with positive people, they lift us up, boost our confidence and make us feel good about ourselves. This can have a significant impact on our self-esteem and overall happiness.

Reduces stress: Surrounding ourselves with supportive people helps us manage stress, as we feel a sense of comfort and security knowing that we have people who will support us in difficult times.

Helps us achieve our goals: Positive and supportive people encourage and motivate us to reach our goals. They provide us with guidance and support, helping us to overcome challenges along the way.

Improves our mental health: Studies have shown that social support can help prevent depression and anxiety and improve overall mental health. When we have positive relationships, we feel more fulfilled and happy, which positively impacts our mental well-being.

How to Surround Yourself with Positive and Supportive People

Seek out new relationships: If you are looking to surround yourself with positive and supportive people, start by seeking out new relationships. Join clubs, attend events, or volunteer in your community to meet new people.

Evaluate your current relationships: Take a look at the people in your life and consider which relationships are positive and which are not. Focus on maintaining and strengthening the positive relationships, and limiting time with those who are not supportive.

Be a positive and supportive person: Attracting positive and supportive people into your life starts with becoming a positive and supportive person yourself. Be kind, understanding, and encouraging to others, and people will naturally be drawn to you.

Surround yourself with like-minded individuals: Seek out people who share your interests, values, and goals. This can help you build stronger, more meaningful relationships with others.

Focus on quality over quantity: It is better to have a few close, positive relationships than a large number of superficial ones. Invest time and effort into developing strong, supportive relationships with those who matter most to you.

Chapter 9

Stay disciplined and persistent

Success is something that many people strive for, but only a few are able to achieve it. While there are many different factors that contribute to success, one of the most important is staying disciplined and persistent. In this article, we will explore what it means to be disciplined and persistent, and why these traits are so important for success.

Discipline is defined as the practice of training people to obey rules or a code of behavior, using punishment to correct disobedience. When it comes to achieving success, discipline means having the self-control to stick to a routine, even when it is difficult or uncomfortable. This means setting goals, developing a plan, and following through on that plan, no matter what obstacles may arise.

Persistence, on the other hand, is the quality of continuing in a course of action even in the face of difficulty or delay in achieving success. It is the willingness to keep trying, even when it seems like progress is slow or there are setbacks along the way.

Together, discipline and persistence are the key ingredients to success. Without discipline, it is easy to get sidetracked or give up when things get tough. Without persistence, it is easy to lose motivation and give up when progress is slow or when obstacles arise.

One of the keys to staying disciplined and persistent is having a clear vision of what you want to achieve. When you have a clear and compelling goal, it is easier to stay motivated and focused, even when the going gets tough. This is why it is so important to set specific, measurable, and achievable goals for yourself.

Another key to staying disciplined and persistent is having a support system. Surrounding yourself with positive and supportive people can provide you with the encouragement and motivation you need to stay on track. This can be as simple as talking to friends or family members, or working with a coach or mentor who can provide guidance and support.

Finally, it is important to develop a positive mindset. This means focusing on what you can do, rather than what you cannot do. It means being proactive, taking ownership of your actions, and being responsible for your own success. By focusing on what you can control, and letting go of what you cannot control, you can stay motivated and focused, even when the going gets tough.

Chapter 10

Celebrating your progress and successes

Celebrating your progress and successes is an important aspect of personal and professional growth. Recognizing the milestones you have achieved can be a source of motivation, inspiration and happiness. Whether you're an individual or a business, taking time to reflect on your achievements and accomplishments is a great way to stay focused and on track towards your goals.

For individuals, celebrating progress and success can help build self-confidence and self-esteem. By reflecting on what you have accomplished, you can feel proud of yourself and your abilities. This, in turn, can give you the motivation to keep pushing forward and to reach your full potential. By celebrating your successes, you can also give yourself a mental break from the hard work and stress that comes with pursuing your goals.

For businesses, celebrating progress and success can be a way to boost employee morale and engagement. When employees feel valued and recognized for their contributions, they are more likely to be motivated and productive. This, in turn, can help a business to achieve its goals more efficiently and effectively. Celebrating success also gives employees a sense of unity and a common goal, which can improve teamwork and collaboration within the company.

There are many ways to celebrate progress and success, depending on the situation. For individuals, it can be as simple as acknowledging your achievements and taking time to reflect on them. You can write them down in a journal, share them with friends and family, or even treat yourself to a small reward. For businesses, celebrations can be as elaborate as a company-wide event or as simple as a team lunch or small gathering.

Celebrating progress and success is an important aspect of personal and professional growth. It helps build self-confidence and motivation, as well as boost employee morale and engagement. By taking time to reflect on your achievements and accomplishments, you can stay focused and motivated on your journey towards your goals. So, go ahead and take the time to celebrate your successes today.

Here are some key things to keep in mind when celebrating your progress and successes:

Be specific: Celebrate specific milestones, achievements, and successes. For example, if you reached a sales goal, or completed a difficult project, take time to acknowledge and celebrate that accomplishment.

Be authentic: Celebrate in a way that is meaningful to you. Don't do things just because others are doing them, or because you feel like you have to. Find a way to celebrate that is authentic and true to who you are.

Share your success: Share your accomplishments with others. This can help you build a network of support, and it can also help you inspire others.

Celebrate others: Take the time to celebrate the successes of those around you. When you celebrate the successes of others, you create a positive and supportive environment that can help everyone thrive.

Be consistent: Celebrate your progress and successes regularly. Don't wait until you have achieved a big goal to celebrate. Celebrate small victories along the way, and make

sure to recognize the effort and hard
work that went into those successes